THESE
SMALL
STONES

THESE SMALL STONES

POEMS SELECTED BY

Norma Farber

A N D

Myra Cohn Livingston

Harper & Row, Publishers

Designed by Trish Parcell Watts
10 9 8 7 6 5 4 3 2 1
First Edition

Library of Congress Cataloging-in-Publication Data
These small stones.

"A Charlotte Zolotow book."
Includes indexes.
Summary: An anthology of poems about the small things
of the real and imagined world that are special in their
own way.
1. Children's poetry.   I. Livingston, Myra Cohn.
PN6109.97.T48 1987   808.81'0088054   87-264
ISBN 0-06-024013-X
ISBN 0-06-024014-8 (lib. bdg.)

For Norma, her children, and her grandchildren
—M.C.L.

Table of Contents

In My Hand

As I picked it up
    to cage it . . .
      the firefly
lit my finger-tips

TAIGI

Translated by Peter Beilenson

Lighting a Fire

One quick scratch
Of a kitchen match
And giant flames unzip!

How do they store
So huge a roar
In such a tiny tip?

X. J. KENNEDY

Jumping Bean

A jumping bean
           is not a bean
I mean
Of course
           it is a bean
It's just that it's not just a bean
But something else as well (unseen).

A caterpillar
           (quite unseen)
Lives inside
           the jumping bean
And when the caterpillar bumps
Itself against the bean
           It jumps!*

* This caterpillar that I mean
  (Which hides inside the jumping bean
  And makes it hop upon the shelf)
  Must be quite full of beans itself!

MARY ANN HOBERMAN

Marbles

Marbles picked up
Heavy by the handful
And held, weighed,
Hard, glossy,
Glassy, cold,
Then poured clicking,
Water-smooth, back
To their bag, seem
Treasure: round jewels,
Slithering gold.

VALERIE WORTH

Old Mother Twitchett has but one eye,
And a long tail which she can let fly,
And every time she goes over a gap,
She leaves a bit of her tail in a trap.

(A needle and thread)

NURSERY RIDDLE

Paperclips

A jumbled sight,
The sheets I write—
    High time for paperclips
To take a bite
And clasp them tight
    Between bright bulldog lips!

X. J. KENNEDY

Safety Pin

Closed, it sleeps
On its side
Quietly,
The silver
Image
Of some
Small fish;

Opened, it snaps
Its tail out
Like a thin
Shrimp, and looks
At the sharp
Point with a
Surprised eye.

VALERIE WORTH

The Snowflake

Before I melt,
Come, look at me!
This lovely icy filigree!
Of a great forest
In one night
I make a wilderness
Of white:
By skyey cold
Of crystals made,
All softly, on
Your finger laid,
I pause, that you
My beauty see:
Breathe, and I vanish
Instantly.

WALTER DE LA MARE

The Tin Frog

I have hopped, when properly wound up,
    the whole length
Of the hallway; once hopped halfway down
    the stairs, and fell.
Since then the two halves of my tin
    have been awry; my strength
Is not quite what it used to be; I do not hop
    so well.

RUSSELL HOBAN

Snail

They have brought me a snail.

Inside it sings
a map-green ocean.
My heart
swells with water,
with small fish
of brown and silver.

They have brought me a snail.

FEDERICO GARCÍA LORCA

Translated by William Jay Smith

On the Ground

Crab

With that crude roof overhead
it's hard to keep one's balance
as he walks swinging his arms
no taller than a bowl
dragging along at his waist
a drawer full of tools

FRANÇOIS DODAT

Translated by Bert and Odette Meyers

Beach Stones

When these small
stones
were
in clear pools and
nets of weed

tide-tumbled
teased by spray

they glowed
moonsilver,
glinted sunsparks on
their speckled
skins.

Spilled on the
shelf
they were
wet-sand jewels
wave-green
still flecked with
foam.

Now
gray stones
lie
dry and dim.

Why did we bring them home?

LILIAN MOORE

Ladybug

A tiny island
appears on your finger
prudently she moves
her neat pebble
see on her back the coins
she carries to heaven.

FRANÇOIS DODAT

Translated by Bert and Odette Meyers

Little Things

Little things, that run, and quail,
And die, in silence and despair!

Little things, that fight, and fail,
And fall, on sea, and earth, and air!

All trapped and frightened little things,
The mouse, the coney, hear our prayer!

As we forgive those done to us,
—The lamb, the linnet, and the hare—

Forgive us all our trespasses,
Little creatures, everywhere!

JAMES STEPHENS

Seeking in my hut
   for unlocked
   midnight treasures . . .
a cricket burglar

Issa

Translated by Peter Beilenson

Small, Smaller

I thought that I knew all there was to know
Of being small, until I saw once, black against
   the snow,
A shrew, trapped in my footprint, jump and fall
And jump again and fall, the hole too deep, the
   walls too tall.

Russell Hoban

Snow Print Two: Hieroglyphics

In the alley
under the last cold rung
of the fire escape
birds are printing
the new snow
with a narrow alphabet.

Their scribbled secrets
tell of lost songs
and the howling wind
that claws like a cat.

These are messages
from the small dark birds
to me.

BARBARA JUSTER ESBENSEN

The Toadstool Wood

The toadstool wood is dark and mouldy,
　　And has a ferny smell.
About the trees hangs something quiet
　　And queer—like a spell.

Beneath the arching sprays of bramble
　　Small creatures make their holes;
Over the moss's close green velvet
　　The stilted spider strolls.

The stalks of toadstools pale and slender
　　That grow from that old log.
Bars they might be to imprison
　　A prince turned to a frog.

There lives no mumbling witch nor wizard
　　In this uncanny place,
Yet you might think you saw at twilight
　　A little, crafty face.

JAMES REEVES

The Sandpiper

Look at the little sandpiper
skittering along the sandy shore
such a little light thing
such a little bright thing
stencilling tiny clawprints
waves will wash away
                    once more.

CHARLOTTE ZOLOTOW

Crickets

all busy punching tickets,
clicking their little punches.
The tickets come in bunches,
good for a brief excursion,
good for a cricket's version
of travel (before it snows) to
the places a cricket goes to.
Alas! the crickets sing alas
in the dry September grass.
Alas, alas, in every acre,
every one a ticket-taker.

DAVID McCORD

In the Air

Firefly: A SONG

A little light is going by,
Is going up to see the sky,
A little light with wings.

I never could have thought of it,
To have a little bug all lit
And made to go on wings.

ELIZABETH MADOX ROBERTS

From: *Bestiary*

Fleas interest me so much
that I let them bite me for hours.
They are perfect, ancient, Sanskrit,
machines that admit of no appeal.
They do not bite to eat,
they bite only to jump;
they are the dancers of the celestial sphere,
delicate acrobats
in the softest and most profound circus;
let them gallop on my skin,
divulge their emotions,
amuse themselves with my blood,
but someone should introduce them to me.
I want to know them closely,
I want to know what to rely on.

PABLO NERUDA

Translated by Elsa Neuberger

For a companion
   on my walking
      trip . . . perhaps
a little butterfly

SHIKI

Translated by Peter Beilenson

Gently, gently, the wind blows
      dandelions' parachutes
into the afternoon sun.

KAZUE MIZUMURA

Green Riders

When there's hardly a breath of wind to stir
The pasture grass and juniper,
Yet they rise and fall like green sea tides
Showing their hidden silver sides,
Then you may know the Elves are near,
You may hear their horns blow faint and clear,
Or see an Elfin Rider pass
Straddling each green and bending grass.

RACHEL FIELD

Little Bird

Little bird, little bird
stay!
there is no voice in the orchard
no moving shadow
other than yours.
Do not leave me now
I stand in stone
heart halted.
Little bird, little bird
sing me my sorrow
Stay!

JULIA CUNNINGHAM

Math Class

She talks about the decimal point,
The reasons why—
But on the window, buzzing free,
A fly

With two red eyes
Moves slowly up the pane.
She moves the decimal one place left
And then again

The fly moves up
And up, practiced and slow.
What I have learned of decimal points
Flies know.

MYRA COHN LIVINGSTON

Mosquitoes

They are born in the swamps of sleeplessness.
They are a viscous blackness which wings about.
Little frail vampires,
miniature dragonflies,
small picadors
with the devil's own sting.

JOSÉ EMILIO PACHECO

Translated by Alastair Reid

A Shower of Cobwebs

Not single filmy threads
floating in the air in all directions,
but perfect flakes or rags,
some near an inch broad and five or six long,
a continual succession of fresh flakes,
twinkling like stars
as they turned their sides to the sun.

GILBERT WHITE

Winter's Tale

After a bitter cold night
of ear-biting snow-fall,
every sensible tan
sycamore ball
puts on a white
angora tam-o'-shanter.

NORMA FARBER

Outside

Glowworm

He studies very late
inside his lamp
prisoner
in a cell of grass
a single star teaches him
how small he is
next to a drop at midnight

FRANÇOIS DODAT
Translated by Bert and Odette Meyers

Jacaranda

On the tree, a peal
of tiny bells . . . on the ground,
lavender litter.

MYRA COHN LIVINGSTON

Acorn

An acorn
Fits perfectly
Into its shingled
Cup, with a stick
Attached
At the top,

Its polished
Nut curves
In the shape
Of a drop, drawn
Down to a thorn
At the tip,

And its heart
Holds folded
Thick white fat
From which
A marvelous
Tree grows up:

I think no better
Invention or
Mechanical trick
Could ever
Be bought
In a shop.

VALERIE WORTH

Hurt no living thing:
   Ladybird, nor butterfly,
Nor moth with dusty wing,
   Nor cricket chirping cheerily,
Nor grasshopper so light of leap,
   Nor dancing gnat, nor beetle fat,
Nor harmless worms that creep.

CHRISTINA ROSSETTI

Buds

When all the other leaves are gone
The brown oak leaves still linger on,
Their branches obstinately lifted
To frozen wind and snow deep-drifted.

But when the winter is well passed
The brown oak leaves drop down at last,
To let the little buds appear
No larger than a mouse's ear.

ELIZABETH COATSWORTH

Seeds

A row of pearls
Delicate green
Cased in white velvet—
The broad bean.

Smallest of birds
Winged and brown,
Seed of the maple
Flutters down.

Cupped like an egg
Without a yolk,
Grows the acorn,
Seed of the oak.

Autumn the housewife
Now unlocks
Seeds of the poppy
In their spice-box.

Silver hair
From an old man's crown
Wind-stolen
Is thistledown.

JAMES REEVES

The Minimal

I study the lives on a leaf: the little
Sleepers, numb nudgers in cold dimensions,
Beetles in caves, newts, stone-deaf fishes,
Lice tethered to long limp subterranean weeds,
Squirmers in bogs,
And bacterial creepers
Wriggling through wounds
Like elvers in ponds,
Their wan mouths kissing the warm sutures,
Cleaning and caressing,
Creeping and healing.

THEODORE ROETHKE

The Snail

At sunset, when the night-dews fall,
Out of the ivy on the wall
With horns outstretched and pointed tail
Comes the grey and noiseless snail.
On ivy stems she clambers down,
Carrying her house of brown.
Safe in the dark, no greedy eye
Can her tender body spy,
While she herself, a hungry thief,
Searches out the freshest leaf.
She travels on as best she can
Like a toppling caravan.

JAMES REEVES

Well! Hello down there,
friend snail! When did you arrive
in such a hurry?

ISSA

Translated by Harry Behn

Who tossed those golden coins,
The dandelions glittering
On my lawn?

KAZUE MIZUMURA

On the Table

Bye Baby Walnut

Walnut in a walnut shell,
what a tiny wizened tot!
Cradle fits him very well—
till he wants a wider cot.

NORMA FARBER

Exactly

She spent the day counting how many birds
    came
to the new feeder and how many seeds they ate.
First she counted the number of seeds in the
Wildbird Mix and at sundown she counted how
    many
seeds were left, subtracted this from that to get
the total sum. It is important to be exact.

ROBERTA METZ

From Table Isle
By Kashima Crag
You gathered baby cockles.
You took them home
And with a stone
You smashed their tiny shells.
In the swift stream
You washed the fish,
Rubbed them with ocean salt.
Rub-a-rub-rub.
Rub-a-rub-rub.
Put them in a tub,
Put them in a pot
And served them up on the table.
They're for your mama, eh,
Darling little girl?
They're for your papa, eh,
Darling little pet?

Anonymous

Noto, Japan
8th century
Translated by Geoffrey Bownas and Anthony Thwaite

In marble halls as white as milk,
Lined with a skin as soft as silk,
Within a fountain crystal-clear,
A golden apple doth appear.
No doors there are to this stronghold,
Yet thieves break in and steal the gold.

(An egg)

NURSERY RIDDLE

Oak Leaf Plate

Oak leaf plate
Acorn cup
Raindrop tea
Drink it up!

Sand for salt
Mud for pie
Twiggy chops
Fine to fry.

Sticks for bread
Stones for meat
Grass for greens
Time to eat!

MARY ANN HOBERMAN

The Little Brown Celery

As it wanders
through
the grisly forests
of the kitchen-garden,

the little brown
celery
is accustomed
to sing:

Three bare
patches in
the cabbage-bed.
Three bare

caterpillars
learning to
fly.
Cabbage-white,

cabbage-white,
soar in the sky.
I shall be a salad
before I die.

GEORGE MACBETH

Salt

Salt for white
And salt for pure.
What's salted right
Will keep and cure.

Salt for cheap
And salt for free.
The poor may reap
Salt from the sea.

Salt for taste
And salt for wit.
Be wise. Don't waste
A pinch of it.

ROBERT FRANCIS

There was an old person of Dean
Who dined on one pea, and one bean;
    For he said, "More than that,
    Would make me too fat."
That cautious old person of Dean.

EDWARD LEAR

The Woman Cleaning Lentils

A lentil, a lentil, a lentil, a stone.
A lentil, a lentil, a lentil, a stone.
A green one, a black one, a green one, a black.
    A stone.
A lentil, a lentil, a stone, a lentil, a lentil, a word.
    Suddenly a word. A lentil.
A lentil, a word, a word next to another
    word. A sentence.
A word, a word, a word, a nonsense speech.
Then an old song.
Then an old dream.
A life, another life, a hard life. A lentil. A life.
An easy life. A hard life. Why easy? Why hard?
Lives next to each other. A life. A word. A lentil.
A green one, a black one, a green one,
    a black one, pain.
A green song, a green lentil, a black one, a stone.
A lentil, a stone, a stone, a lentil.

ZEHRD

Translated by Diana der Hovanessian and Marzbed Margossian

Mouse Dinner

A mouse doesn't dine
on potatoes and beef . . .
he nibbles the seeds
from a pod or a sheaf.

He catches a beetle
and then gives a brief
little wipe of his mouth
on a napkin of leaf.

AILEEN FISHER

A Piece of It All

Burning Bright

A mermaid's tears
have silver fish in them,
a tiger's,
yellow stars.
Mine have spikes
and spokes of bikes
and yours
have blue guitars.

LILLIAN MORRISON

Flower in the Crannied Wall

Flower in the crannied wall,
I pluck you out of the crannies,
I hold you here, root and all, in my hand,
Little flower—but *if* I could understand
What you are, root and all, and all in all,
I should know what God and man is.

ALFRED, LORD TENNYSON

How soft a Caterpillar steps—
I find one on my Hand
From such a velvet world it comes
Such plushes at command
Its soundless travels just arrest
My slow—terrestrial eye
Intent upon its own career
What use has it for me—

EMILY DICKINSON

My Toe

My toe
is only
a little part of me
and
way
down T
     H
     E
     R
     E

So
why
should I care
if it should hurt me?
It certainly
would not be
very trying
would it?
Then why
am I
crying?

FELICE HOLMAN

(sitting in a tree-)
o small you
sitting in a tree-

sitting in a treetop

riding on a greenest

riding on a greener
(o little i)
riding on a leaf

o least who
sing small thing
dance little joy

(shine most prayer)

e. e. cummings

From: *Square as a House*

If you could be small
Would you be a mouse
Or a mouse's child
Or a mouse's house
Or a mouse's house's
Front door key?
Who would you
Which would you
What would you be?

KARLA KUSKIN

Things on a Microscope Slide

Your sore-throat germ may say, "Heh heh,
I'm little! I can hide!"
Till a doctor grabs it by the tail
And slings it on a slide,

A kind of flat glass-bottomed ark
Where he collects, this Noah,
The eyes of flies, the knees of fleas,
The toes of protozoa.

X. J. Kennedy

Thumbs

Oh the thumb-sucker's thumb
May look wrinkled and wet
And withered, and white as the snow,
But the taste of a thumb
Is the sweetest taste yet
(As only we thumb-suckers know).

SHEL SILVERSTEIN

Who Am I?

The trees ask me,
And the sky,
And the sea asks me
      Who am I?

The grass asks me,
And the sand,
And the rocks ask me
      Who I am.

The wind tells me
At nightfall,
And the rain tells me
      Someone small.

Someone small
Someone small
But a piece
of
it
all.

FELICE HOLMAN

Trapped Mouse

I found your body, a little purse
of fur and bone, and cradled
what was left, wishing my breath
could lend you life, restart the hum,
restore your chances of another run
through the grasses of your meadow home.
I could not. But when tomorrow comes
I'll lie among the flowers of your field,
willing myself to size you grew to be
and for a little while become
what you once were and squeak the morning in.

JULIA CUNNINGHAM

These Small Stones:

An Afterword

"Every so often," Norma Farber wrote to me in May of 1979, "I think I'd like to try my hand (wing? hoof?) at an anthology. Haven't the stamina. One particular theme keeps recurring to me . . . a collection of poems about all sorts of small things. The subject has haunted me for a long time. . . . I'd love to read such an anthology & wish you'd consider editing it. I enclose a few examples I once gathered in a gung-ho mood!"

Norma, whom I had met briefly in Boston in 1978, had been sending me her own poetry for use in several anthologies I was compiling. "Your idea for an anthology," I replied, "has not, to my knowledge, been done. How about doing it *with* me? Had you ever considered a collaboration? Just now I'm up to the top of the room with work, so give it some thought—couldn't manage until the fall at the very first."

A year later Norma was still gathering poems about the small. We were both busy, but our enthusiasm continued. "I trust you'll tell me quite directly," she wrote in January of 1981, "if you're too deeply involved with other commitments. . . . In that case, perhaps I should be trying to market a collection of my own poems, *Still Small Voices* . . . though I'd prefer the challenge of collaborating with you. Well, let me know your interest and timetable."

It was September of 1981 before I commented on the last fifty poems Norma had found and sent her, in return,

73

others I liked. We met for dinner in Boston that November to discuss her newest "clutch of smalls." I remember speaking with her about an anthology's need for balance in terms of poets, subject, viewpoint, and appeal to young readers. We were both excited about the project, but other work was more pressing. "Trust you have been receiving the sundries I send," she wrote in September of 1983. In November we had a brief visit at the home of Paul and Ethel Heins outside Boston. The anthology, I assured her, was still in work. I returned home to California to learn, a few weeks later, that she was ill. No further batches of her favorite poems were sent. The anthology came to a standstill. Norma died in March of 1984.

But hundreds of poems still remained to be read. The box on the shelf containing all we had gathered haunted me more frequently. I did not wish Norma's love for small things to be forgotten; I finished the anthology. When her poem *All Those Mothers at the Manger* was published as a picture book in the fall of 1985, I contacted her son Tom, who lives in Berkeley, California, and Charlotte Zolotow at Harper & Row in New York. We all believed that Norma's idea should live.

Authors oftentimes have working titles as they think about their books. For Norma the title was *Long Live the Small*, which she took from a poem by Henri Fabré. For me it was *Small Things*. Charlotte, most imaginatively, chose *These Small Stones*, a title and image that surely would have delighted Norma as well as those who may find in this anthology their own small sundries, their own discoveries. This, I believe, is what Norma would have wished.

M.C.L.

January 1987

INDEX OF AUTHORS AND TRANSLATORS

INDEX OF FIRST LINES

Old Mother Twitchett has but one eye, 7
On the tree, a peal, 37
One quick scratch, 4

Salt for white, 56
Seeking in my hut, 20
She spent the day counting how many birds came, 50
She talks about the decimal point, 32
(sitting in a tree-), 66

The toadstool wood is dark and mouldy, 22
The trees ask me, 70
There was an old person of Dean, 56

They are born in the swamps of sleeplessness., 33
They have brought me a snail., 12

Walnut in a walnut shell, 49
Well! Hello down there, 46
When all the other leaves are gone, 41
When there's hardly a breath of wind to stir, 30
When these small, 16
Who tossed those golden coins, 46
With that crude roof overhead, 15

Your sore-throat germ may say, "Heh heh, 68

INDEX OF TITLES

ACKNOWLEDGMENTS

Every effort has been made to trace the ownership of all copyrighted material and to secure the necessary permissions to reprint these selections. In the event of any question arising as to the use of any material, the editor and the publisher, while expressing regret for any inadvertent error, will be happy to make the necessary correction in future printings. Thanks are due to the following for permission to reprint the copyrighted materials listed below:

Atheneum Publishers, Inc., for: X. J. Kennedy, "Lighting a Fire" from *The Forgetful Wishing Well.* Copyright © 1985 X. J. Kennedy. (A Margaret K. McElderry Book.) Myra Cohn Livingston, "Jacaranda" from *Monkey Puzzles and Other Poems.* Copyright © 1984 Myra Cohn Livingston. (A Margaret K. McElderry Book). Myra Cohn Livingston, "Math Class" from *The Malibu and Other Poems.* Copyright © 1972 Myra Cohn Livingston. (A Margaret K. McElderry Book.) George MacBeth, "The Little Brown Celery" from *Shrapnel and a Poet's Year*; Anthony Sheil Associates, Ltd. for the Canadian rights. Copyright © 1973 George MacBeth. Lilian Moore, "Beach Stones" from *Something New Begins.* Copyright © 1982 Lilian Moore. All reprinted with the permission of Atheneum Publishers, Inc.

Columbia University Press, for: "Mosquitoes" by José Emilio Pacheco, from *Don't Ask Me How the Time Goes By.* Translated by Alastair Reid. Copyright © 1978. "The Woman Cleaning Lentils" by Zehrd, from *Anthology of Armenian Poetry.* Translated by Diana der Hovanessian and Marzbed Margossian. Copyright © 1978. Reprinted by permission of Columbia University Press.

Julia Cunningham, for "Little Bird" and "Trapped Mouse," copyright © 1987 by Julia Cunningham. Used by permission of the author.

Dodd, Mead & Company, Inc., for "There Was an Old Person of Dean" by Edward Lear, from *The Complete Nonsense Book.*

Doubleday & Company, Inc., for "The Minimal," copyright 1942 by Theodore Roethke from *The Collected Poems of Theodore Roethke.* Reprinted by permission of Doubleday & Company, Inc.

Tom Farber, for: "Bye Baby Walnut" from *Small Wonders* by Norma Farber, published by Coward, McCann & Geoghegan, Inc. Copyright